Be A Pin

Stand Tall
Wear A Crown
& Be Sweet
On The Inside

Daily Gratitude Journal with
100 Affirmations for Being
Thankful and Happy

This Notebook Belongs To:

BRENDA ♡

E-mail:

Phone:

Lightly ruled pages with daily
gratitude lists, and gratitude
prompts.

Year 2017

January

Su	M	Tu	W	Th	F	Sa
1	2	3	4	5	6	7
8	9	10	11	12	13	14
15	16	17	18	19	20	21
22	23	24	25	26	27	28
29	30	31				

February

Su	M	Tu	W	Th	F	Sa
			1	2	3	4
5	6	7	8	9	10	11
12	13	14	15	16	17	18
19	20	21	22	23	24	25
26	27	28				

March

Su	M	Tu	W	Th	F	Sa
			1	2	3	4
5	6	7	8	9	10	11
12	13	14	15	16	17	18
19	20	21	22	23	24	25
26	27	28	29	30	31	

April

Su	M	Tu	W	Th	F	Sa
						1
2	3	4	5	6	7	8
9	10	11	12	13	14	15
16	17	18	19	20	21	22
23	24	25	26	27	28	29
30						

May

Su	M	Tu	W	Th	F	Sa
	1	2	3	4	5	6
7	8	9	10	11	12	13
14	15	16	17	18	19	20
21	22	23	24	25	26	27
28	29	30	31			

June

Su	M	Tu	W	Th	F	Sa
				1	2	3
4	5	6	7	8	9	10
11	12	13	14	15	16	17
18	19	20	21	22	23	24
25	26	27	28	29	30	

July

Su	M	Tu	W	Th	F	Sa
						1
2	3	4	5	6	7	8
9	10	11	12	13	14	15
16	17	18	19	20	21	22
23	24	25	26	27	28	29
30	31					

August

Su	M	Tu	W	Th	F	Sa
		1	2	3	4	5
6	7	8	9	10	11	12
13	14	15	16	17	18	19
20	21	22	23	24	25	26
27	28	29	30	31		

September

Su	M	Tu	W	Th	F	Sa
					1	2
3	4	5	6	7	8	9
10	11	12	13	14	15	16
17	18	19	20	21	22	23
24	25	26	27	28	29	30

October

Su	M	Tu	W	Th	F	Sa
1	2	3	4	5	6	7
8	9	10	11	12	13	14
15	16	17	18	19	20	21
22	23	24	25	26	27	28
29	30	31				

November

Su	M	Tu	W	Th	F	Sa
		1	2	3	4	
5	6	7	8	9	10	11
12	13	14	15	16	17	18
19	20	21	22	23	24	25
26	27	28	29	30		

December

Su	M	Tu	W	Th	F	Sa
					1	2
3	4	5	6	7	8	9
10	11	12	13	14	15	16
17	18	19	20	21	22	23
24	25	26	27	28	29	30
31						

Date Event

Date:

I Am Grateful Because:

1.

2.

3.

Today I Will Improve…

I Will Do This By…

What is your favorite activity to do?

I am thankful for every spark of insight that inspires me.

Date:

I Am Grateful Because:

1.

2.

3.

I Will Get Better At...

I Will Do This By...

What small thing that you use daily are you grateful for?

I sincerely appreciate the support I receive from others.

Date:

I Am Grateful Because:	1.
	2.
	3.

I Will Get Better At...

I Will Do This By...

What in nature are you grateful for?

Each Morning I give thanks for another day of life.

Date:

I Am Grateful Because:

1.

2.

3.

I Will Get Better At...

I Will Do This By...

What was the best thing that happened today?

Every day I am becoming more and more grateful for what I have in my life.

Gratitude & Affirmation Journal

Date:

I Am Grateful Because:	1.
	2.
	3.

| I Will Get Better At… | |

| I Will Do This By… | |

What skills or abilities are you thankful to have?

Gratitude is something I just naturally feel all the time.

Date:

I Am Grateful Because:

1.

2.

3.

I Will Get Better At…

I Will Do This By…

What material items are you most grateful for?

I appreciate all others in my life.

Date:

I Am Grateful Because:

1.

2.

3.

I Will Get Better At...

I Will Do This By...

What is one thing you love about yourself?

I am grateful for every experience in my life.

I Am Grateful Because:

1.

2.

3.

I Will Get Better At...

I Will Do This By...

What texture are you grateful for?

Every day I appreciate my life more than ever.

Date:

I Am Grateful Because:	1.
	2.
	3.

I Will Get Better At...

I Will Do This By...

What color are you grateful for?

I am immensely grateful for all the good in my life.

Date:

I Am Grateful Because:	1.
	2.
	3.

I Will Get Better At...	

I Will Do This By...	

When were you were able to help someone else, why are you thankful for that?

My mind is always effortlessly focused on positivity and thankfulness.

Date:

I Am Grateful Because:

1.
2.
3.

I Will Get Better At…

I Will Do This By…

What technology are you grateful for?

I am the kind of person who just always appreciates whatever life brings my way.

I Am Grateful Because:

1.
2.
3.

I Will Get Better At...

I Will Do This By...

What season are you grateful for?

I find it easy to maintain an attitude of gratitude even in difficult situations.

Date:

I Am Grateful Because:	1.
	2.
	3.

I Will Get Better At...

I Will Do This By...

What sight are you grateful for today?

I am deeply grateful for the small acts of kindness given to me.

Date:

I Am Grateful Because:

1.

2.

3.

I Will Get Better At...

I Will Do This By...

What challenge are you grateful for?

I am filled with immense gratitude for all that I have in my life.

Date:

I Am Grateful Because:

1.

2.

3.

I Will Get Better At…

I Will Do This By…

What memory are you grateful for?

My daily attitude is one of gratitude.

Date:

I Am Grateful Because:

1.

2.

3.

I Will Get Better At...

I Will Do This By...

What story are you grateful for?

I deeply appreciate everything I have in my life.

Date:

I Am Grateful Because:	1.
	2.
	3.

| I Will Get Better At… | |

| I Will Do This By… | |

Who is someone you have never met that you are grateful for?

I sincerely appreciate all the help I receive from others.

Date:

I Am Grateful Because:

1.

2.

3.

I Will Get Better At...

I Will Do This By...

What is something beautiful that you saw today?

I am grateful for the expanding journey that unfolds before me.

Date:

I Am Grateful Because:	1.
	2.
	3.

| I Will Get Better At… | |

| I Will Do This By… | |

What piece of art are you grateful for?

I pay tribute to my being by living each day as powerfully and positively as I can.

Date:

I Am Grateful Because:

1.

2.

3.

I Will Get Better At...

I Will Do This By...

What place are you most grateful for?

I appreciate all forms of life on this planet.

Date:

I Am Grateful Because:

1.

2.

3.

I Will Get Better At…

I Will Do This By…

What freedoms are you grateful for?

It is my greatest desire to live each and every day with unlimited gratitude.

Date:

I Am Grateful Because:

1.

2.

3.

I Will Get Better At...

I Will Do This By...

What foods are you most thankful for?

My grateful heart attracts more of everything I appreciate in life.

Date:

I Am Grateful Because:

1.

2.

3.

I Will Get Better At...

I Will Do This By...

Who has recently done something to help you, how can you thank them?

I practice the feeling of gratitude every day.

Date:

I Am Grateful Because:

1.

2.

3.

I Will Get Better At...

I Will Do This By...

What knowledge are you grateful for?

I am thankful for simply being alive.

Date:

I Am Grateful Because:	1.
	2.
	3.

I Will Get Better At…

I Will Do This By…

What is a song you're thankful to be able to listen to, why?

I just naturally have an attitude of gratitude.

Date:

I Am Grateful Because:

1.

2.

3.

I Will Get Better At...

I Will Do This By...

Who in your life are you grateful for?

I am forever grateful for the miraculous life energy in my body.

Gratitude & Affirmation Journal

Date:

I Am Grateful Because:

1.

2.

3.

I Will Get Better At...

I Will Do This By...

What do you love about your parents?

I am grateful to everyone who has brought positive energy into my life.

Date:

I Am Grateful Because:	1.
	2.
	3.

| I Will Get Better At... | |

| I Will Do This By... | |

What achievements in your life have brought you the most happiness?

I greet this new day with abundant gratitude.

Gratitude & Affirmation Journal

Date:

I Am Grateful Because:

1.

2.

3.

I Will Get Better At...

I Will Do This By...

What small thing that happened today are you grateful for?

I am deeply grateful for each experience life brings me.

Date:

I Am Grateful Because:

1.

2.

3.

I Will Get Better At…

I Will Do This By…

Who in your life is hard to get along with, write down one quality in them you are grateful for.

Gratitude is a habit that I nurture every day.

Date:

I Am Grateful Because:

1.

2.

3.

I Will Get Better At...

I Will Do This By...

What form of expression are you most grateful for?

I accept all gifts graciously and with deep gratitude.

Date:

I Am Grateful Because:

1.

2.

3.

I Will Get Better At...

I Will Do This By...

What tradition are you grateful for?

I remind myself of all life's blessings every day.

Gratitude & Affirmation Journal

Date:

I Am Grateful Because:	1.
	2.
	3.

| I Will Get Better At... | |
| | |

| I Will Do This By... | |
| | |

What made you laugh today?

The universe supports me and all my desires.

I Am Grateful Because:

1.
2.
3.

I Will Get Better At...

I Will Do This By...

What challenge have you overcome that has made you stronger?

I am filled with immense gratitude for....

Date:

I Am Grateful Because:	1.
	2.
	3.

| I Will Get Better At… | |
| | |

| I Will Do This By… | |
| | |

What is a sound you are grateful for?

I see the beauty in nature that surrounds me.

I Am Grateful Because:

1.

2.

3.

I Will Get Better At...

I Will Do This By...

What is something you love in nature?

I am grateful for all the good in my life.

Date:

I Am Grateful Because:	1.
	2.
	3.

I Will Get Better At...

I Will Do This By...

Which of your five senses are you most grateful for?

I appreciate every experience in my life.

I Am Grateful Because:

1.

2.

3.

I Will Get Better At...

I Will Do This By...

What is a special memory from childhood?

I choose to appreciate everything life brings me.

Date:

I Am Grateful Because:	1.
	2.
	3.

| I Will Get Better At… | |

| I Will Do This By… | |

What abilities are you grateful for?

I feel an abundance of gratitude for everything I have and receive every day.

Date:

I Am Grateful Because:

1.

2.

3.

I Will Get Better At...

I Will Do This By...

What activities and hobbies would you miss if you were unable to do them?

I am grateful for the ability to turn inward and find peace.

Date:

I Am Grateful Because:

1.
2.
3.

I Will Get Better At…

I Will Do This By…

What is something you are good at?

I am forever grateful for being able to contribute to the lives of others.

Date:

I Am Grateful Because:	1.
	2.
	3.

I Will Get Better At...

I Will Do This By...

What talent or skill do you have that you are grateful for?

I am very grateful that I am able to reprogram my life for the better.

Date:

I Am Grateful Because:

1.

2.

3.

I Will Get Better At...

I Will Do This By...

What food are you most grateful for?

I have an attitude of gratitude.

I Am Grateful Because:

1.

2.

3.

I Will Get Better At...

I Will Do This By...

What about your body are you grateful for?

I thank people often.

Date:

I Am Grateful Because:

1.

2.

3.

I Will Get Better At…

I Will Do This By…

What part of your morning routine are you most thankful for?

Every day I give thanks for all that blesses my life.

Date:

I Am Grateful Because:

1.
2.
3.

I Will Get Better At…

I Will Do This By…

What kindness did see someone perform today?

I am grateful for my limitless inner resources.

Date:

I Am Grateful Because:

1.

2.

3.

I Will Get Better At…

I Will Do This By…

What do you like about this time of year?

I am so grateful for every person and every thing in my life.

Date:

Be A Pineapple

	1.
I Am Grateful Because:	2.
	3.

| **I Will Get Better At...** | |

| **I Will Do This By...** | |

What do you take for granted about your day to day experience that you can be thankful for?

My thoughts are focused on positivity and thankfulness.

Date:

I Am Grateful Because:

1.

2.

3.

I Will Get Better At...

I Will Do This By...

What travel experience/vacation are you most thankful for?

I am grateful to the universe for helping me so solve my problems.

I Am Grateful Because:

1.

2.

3.

I Will Get Better At...

I Will Do This By...

What is a smell that you are grateful for?

I radiate supreme gratitude for every positive result in my life.

Gratitude & Affirmation Journal

Date:

I Am Grateful Because:	1.
	2.
	3.

I Will Get Better At...

I Will Do This By...

What taste are you grateful for?

I readily show my appreciation for others.

Date:

I Am Grateful Because:

1.

2.

3.

I Will Get Better At...

I Will Do This By...

Who are you grateful for, what do you love about them?

I am immensely grateful to be able to create the life I want.

Date:

I Am Grateful Because:	1.
	2.
	3.

I Will Get Better At…

I Will Do This By…

What book are you most grateful for?

I am immensely grateful for the joy my pet brings into my life.

Date:

I Am Grateful Because:	1.
	2.
	3.

I Will Get Better At...

I Will Do This By...

What smell are you grateful for today?

I am grateful for having an open mind with which to receive new ideas.

Gratitude & Affirmation Journal

Date:

I Am Grateful Because:	1.
	2.
	3.

I Will Get Better At…

I Will Do This By…

What song are you most grateful for?

I reflect, with gratitude, on every moment of my life.

Date:

I Am Grateful Because:

1.

2.

3.

I Will Get Better At...

I Will Do This By...

What teacher in your past are you most grateful for?

I am grateful for the power I have over my future.

Gratitude & Affirmation Journal

Date:

I Am Grateful Because:	1.
	2.
	3.

| I Will Get Better At... | |

| I Will Do This By... | |

What do you like about where you live?

I experience gratitude for everything I have in my life.

Date:

Be A Pineapple

I Am Grateful Because:

1.
2.
3.

I Will Get Better At...

I Will Do This By...

What holiday are you grateful for?

Thank you for all the good things in my life!.

Date:

I Am Grateful Because:	1.
	2.
	3.

| I Will Get Better At... | |

| I Will Do This By... | |

What made you smile today?

I count my many blessings each and every day.

Date:

I Am Grateful Because:

1.

2.

3.

I Will Get Better At...

I Will Do This By...

What moment this week are you most grateful for?

Feeling gratitude puts me in a state of calm and openness.

Date:

	1.
I Am Grateful Because:	2.
	3.

I Will Get Better At…

I Will Do This By…

Who is someone who lives far a way that you are grateful for?

I am grateful for who I am and what I have.

Date:

I Am Grateful Because:	1.
	2.
	3.

I Will Get Better At...

I Will Do This By...

What gift did you love receiving this year?

I am blessed.

Date:

I Am Grateful Because:	1.
	2.
	3.

| I Will Get Better At… | |

| I Will Do This By… | |

What is a unique experience you've had that you are thankful for?

I am grateful for all that the universe gives me.

I Am Grateful Because:

1.
2.
3.

I Will Get Better At...

I Will Do This By...

What sound are you grateful for today?

I pay my bills with gratitude.

Date:

I Am Grateful Because:	1.
	2.
	3.

I Will Get Better At…	

I Will Do This By…	

What taste are you grateful for today?

I clearly see the beauty of life that flourishes around me.

I Am Grateful Because:	1.
	2.
	3.

I Will Get Better At…

I Will Do This By…

What is something that was hard to do but you did it anyway?

I am grateful for who I am and the time that I am living in.

Date:

I Am Grateful Because:

1.

2.

3.

I Will Get Better At...

I Will Do This By...

What aspects of your work are you thankful for?

I repeatedly give thanks for all the good things in my life.

Date:

I Am Grateful Because:
1.
2.
3.

I Will Get Better At...

I Will Do This By...

What do you love about your best friend?

I gratefully accept all the good that manifests in my life.

Date:

I Am Grateful Because:	1.
	2.
	3.

| I Will Get Better At... | |

| I Will Do This By... | |

What friend/family member are you grateful for today?

I am eternally grateful for all the lessons life teaches me.

Date:

I Am Grateful Because:	1.
	2.
	3.

| I Will Get Better At... | |

| I Will Do This By... | |

What do you like about your job?

Regardless of the weather, I am thankful for another great day.

Date:

I Am Grateful Because:	1.
	2.
	3.

| I Will Get Better At... | |

| I Will Do This By... | |

What spiritual beliefs are you grateful for?

I give thanks for everything I have.

Date:

I Am Grateful Because:
1.
2.
3.

I Will Get Better At…

I Will Do This By…

What is something you're grateful to have learned this week?

My life is full of so many things to be grateful for.

Date:

I Am Grateful Because:	1.
	2.
	3.

I Will Get Better At...

I Will Do This By...

What is different today than a year ago that you are grateful for?

I am thankful for the love and companionship of my pets.

Date:

I Am Grateful Because:	1.
	2.
	3.

| I Will Get Better At... | |

| I Will Do This By... | |

What touch are you grateful for today?

My mind is filled with thoughts of gratitude.

Date:

I Am Grateful Because:	1.
	2.
	3.

| I Will Get Better At… | |

| I Will Do This By… | |

What is a smell that you are grateful for?

I live an attitude of gratitude.

Date:

I Am Grateful Because:	1.
	2.
	3.

| I Will Get Better At... | |

| I Will Do This By... | |

What place are you most grateful for?

I am so grateful for supportive friends and a loving family.

Date:

I Am Grateful Because:	1.
	2.
	3.

| I Will Get Better At… | |
| | |

| I Will Do This By… | |
| | |

What is a special memory from childhood?

I am continually amazed at how abundant my life is already!.

Date:

I Am Grateful Because:

1.

2.

3.

I Will Get Better At…

I Will Do This By…

What friend/family member are you grateful for today?

My life is full of countless blessings.

Date:

I Am Grateful Because:

1.

2.

3.

I Will Get Better At…

I Will Do This By…

What is your favorite activity to do?

I am grateful for all the great health, love, and goodness that my life has revealed to me.

Date:

I Am Grateful Because:

1.

2.

3.

I Will Get Better At…

I Will Do This By…

What foods are you most thankful for?

I am grateful for my inner longing to connect with my soul.

Date:

I Am Grateful Because:	1.
	2.
	3.

I Will Get Better At...	

I Will Do This By...	

What abilities are you grateful for?

I find it easy to take time each day to take a moment and feel sincere gratitude.

Date: _____

Be A Pineapple

I Am Grateful Because:	1.
	2.
	3.

| I Will Get Better At… | |

| I Will Do This By… | |

What technology are you grateful for?

I treat life as the ultimate gift.

Date:

I Am Grateful Because:	1.
	2.
	3.

| I Will Get Better At… | |

| I Will Do This By… | |

What do you love about your parents?

I am eternally grateful for all the pleasure my senses bring me.

Date:

I Am Grateful Because:

1.

2.

3.

I Will Get Better At...

I Will Do This By...

What made you laugh today?

Being grateful for what I have brings more abundance into my life.

Date:

I Am Grateful Because:	1.	
	2.	
	3.	

I Will Get Better At…	

I Will Do This By…	

What skills or abilities are you thankful to have?

I appreciate everything I have in my life and always keep the door open for more blessings.

Date:

I Am Grateful Because:	1.
	2.
	3.

| I Will Get Better At… | |

| I Will Do This By… | |

What sight are you grateful for today?

Every day I thank the universe for the qualities and talents that make me so unique.

Date:

I Am Grateful Because:

1.

2.

3.

I Will Get Better At...

I Will Do This By...

What spiritual beliefs are you grateful for?

I feel grateful each morning for all that I have in my life.

Date:

I Am Grateful Because:

1.

2.

3.

I Will Get Better At...

I Will Do This By...

What teacher in your past are you most grateful for?

Every evening I give thanks for all the blessings in my life.

Date:

I Am Grateful Because:	1.
	2.
	3.

| I Will Get Better At... | |

| I Will Do This By... | |

What is one thing you love about yourself?

I end my day with gratitude and peace.

Date:

I Am Grateful Because:	1.
	2.
	3.

| I Will Get Better At... | |

| I Will Do This By... | |

What smell are you grateful for today?

I am forever grateful for everyone who has provided a positive example in my life.

Date:

I Am Grateful Because:	1.
	2.
	3.

I Will Get Better At...

I Will Do This By...

When were you were able to help someone else, why are you thankful for that?

I deeply appreciate all the people in my life.

Date:

I Am Grateful Because:

1.

2.

3.

I Will Get Better At...

I Will Do This By...

What achievements in your life have brought you the most happiness?

I deeply appreciate all that I have.

Gratitude & Affirmation Journal

Date:

I Am Grateful Because:

1.

2.

3.

I Will Get Better At...

I Will Do This By...

Who are you grateful for, what do you love about them?

I am immensely grateful to be alive today.

Date:

I Am Grateful Because:

1.
2.
3.

I Will Get Better At...

I Will Do This By...

What is something that was hard to do but you did it anyway?

I appreciate everything I have and I show my sincerest gratitude to my loved ones.

Date:

I Am Grateful Because:	1.
	2.
	3.

| I Will Get Better At... | |

| I Will Do This By... | |

What sound are you grateful for today?

I am immensely grateful for all the precious moments in my life.

I Am Grateful Because:

1.
2.
3.

I Will Get Better At…

I Will Do This By…

What holiday are you grateful for?

I take time to be grateful for something as simple as a blue sky or the sound of laughter.

Date:

I Am Grateful Because:	1.
	2.
	3.

| I Will Get Better At... | |

| I Will Do This By... | |

What challenge are you grateful for?

The more I give thanks, the more things I have to be thankful for.

Date:

I Am Grateful Because:

1.

2.

3.

I Will Get Better At...

I Will Do This By...

What activities and hobbies would you miss if you were unable to do them?

I express my faith with gratitude.

Date:

I Am Grateful Because:	1.
	2.
	3.

| I Will Get Better At... | |

| I Will Do This By... | |

What is something you are good at?

I am truly grateful for the abundance now flowing into my life.

I Am Grateful Because:	1.
	2.
	3.

I Will Get Better At…	

I Will Do This By…	

What season are you grateful for?

I end my day with quiet reflection and appreciation.

For more amazing journals and adult colouring books from RW Squared Media, visit:
Amazon.com
CreateSpace.com
RWSquaredMedia.Wordpress.com

She Believed She Could
So She Did
Adult Coloring Book

Cities of the World
Coloring Book for Adults

The Matryoshka Nesting
Doll Coloring Book for
Adults

Start Where You Are
Adult Coloring Book

For more motivational and inspirational shirts, mugs and other items, visit:

www.cafepress.com/SheBelievedSheCould

Made in the USA
Middletown, DE
07 August 2017